HERDING
DOGS

BY NANCY FURSTINGER

CANINE ★ ATHLETES

SportsZone

An Imprint of Abdo Publishing
abdobooks.com

abdobooks.com

Published by Abdo Publishing, a division of ABDO, PO Box 398166, Minneapolis, Minnesota 55439. Copyright © 2019 by Abdo Consulting Group, Inc. International copyrights reserved in all countries. No part of this book may be reproduced in any form without written permission from the publisher. SportsZone™ is a trademark and logo of Abdo Publishing.

Printed in the United States of America, North Mankato, Minnesota
092018
012019

THIS BOOK CONTAINS
RECYCLED MATERIALS

Cover Photos: Laurinson Crusoe/Shutterstock Images, top; iStockphoto, bottom
Interior Photos: iStockphoto, 5, 9 (top right), 9 (bottom left), 9 (bottom right); Bob Pool/ Shutterstock Images, 8; Eric Isselee/Shutterstock Images, 9 (top left); Lisa Nagorskaya/ Shutterstock Images, 11; Holly Kuchera/Shutterstock Images, 13; Sarit Richerson/ Shutterstock Images, 16; Krizek Vaclav/Shutterstock Images, 19; Edwin Remsberg/Alamy, 20; Shutterstock Images, 22, 29; Ben Birchall/PA Images/Alamy, 25; O. Giel/juniors@ wildlife/Juniors Bildarchiv GmbH/Alamy, 26

Editor: Marie Pearson
Series Designer: Craig Hinton

Library of Congress Control Number: 2018949087

Publisher's Cataloging-in-Publication Data

Names: Furstinger, Nancy, author.
Title: Herding dogs / by Nancy Furstinger.
Description: Minneapolis, Minnesota : Abdo Publishing, 2019 | Series: Canine athletes | Includes online resources and index.
Identifiers: ISBN 9781532117381 (lib. bdg.) | ISBN 9781641855952 (pbk) | ISBN 9781532170249 (ebook)
Subjects: LCSH: Dog sports--Juvenile literature. | Herding dogs--Juvenile literature. | Dogs-- Behavior--Juvenile literature. | Dogs--Behavior--Juvenile literature.
Classification: DDC 636.70886--dc23

TABLE OF
CONTENTS

BLUE'S SHEEPDOG TRIAL

A Border collie named Blue dashed through the gates and raced far across the pasture. His black and white fur was a blur. He headed toward a flock of five sheep. Blue's handler yelled out a command from back at the starting point. "Come-bye!" she shouted. Blue circled around the sheep in a clockwise direction. He would need to move the sheep around the course at a steady pace.

Suddenly two sheep split off from the flock. Blue circled behind the stray sheep. "Lie down!" his handler shouted. The Border collie immediately stopped and

Border collies are considered some of the best herding dogs.

lay down on the ground. The two sheep rejoined their flock. Blue sprung back into action as his handler guided the dog with her voice. Dog and handler worked in sync to keep the sheep together. "Good boy," the handler praised Blue.

The Border collie gathered the sheep through two sets of gates and brought them to the handler. Then Blue herded the sheep to a pen. His handler shut the gate.

The audience clapped. Blue had successfully completed the sheepdog trial. He scored 80 points out of 100 and came in third place. Blue had proved that he had the stamina and control for the sport. Herding was in his blood.

HERDING HISTORY

Approximately 10,000 years ago, hunters began herding groups of wild animals. These animals traveled in groups called herds, which helped keep them safe. Sheep, cattle, and goats roamed the grasslands. Herders tamed and controlled the herds. Then they used the animals for meat, milk, and hides.

Ranchers and farmers today still rely on herding dogs to control livestock.

Herders needed help with their herds. They had to guide the herds over large areas while keeping all of the animals together. They also needed to protect the herds from predators such as wolves. So herders began breeding working dogs for these tasks. Farmers still use herding dogs today.

HERDING BREEDS

People have been breeding herding dogs for thousands of years. They breed dogs with desirable traits. These include the instinct to gather a group of animals without attacking them. Herding dogs need to show an eagerness to work with the handler and often bond strongly with that person. They also need to prove that they have the intelligence to make decisions when the handler is out of earshot.

Many countries including the United Kingdom developed herding breeds. These breeds vary in size and have different appearances. But all of the herding breeds can move and control groups of animals while keeping them from straying.

Herding breeds are popular. However, not everyone with a herding dog lives on or near a working farm. That's why herding breed clubs around the world have turned herding into a sport. These clubs hold trials. Different breeds are judged on their herding styles. So even if herding dogs don't have any livestock to work at home, they can keep their instincts sharp through the sport of herding.

BREEDS THAT CAN COMPETE

The American Kennel Club (AKC) recognizes 30 breeds in its herding group. All of these dogs can be entered into herding events. Some breeds not in the herding group, such as Rottweilers and Boxers, can also participate.

COMMON
HERDING BREEDS

AUSTRALIAN SHEPHERD

Height: 18–23 inches
(46–58 cm)
Weight: 40–65 pounds
(20–29 kg)

PEMBROKE WELSH CORGI

Height: 10–12 inches
(25–30 cm)
Weight: up to 30 pounds
(14 kg)

GERMAN SHEPHERD

Height: 22–26 inches
(56–66 cm)
Weight: 50–90 pounds
(25–40 kg)

BORDER COLLIE

Height: 18–22 inches
(46–56 cm)
Weight: 30–55 pounds
(14–25 kg)

STARTING
THE SPORT

Sheepdog trials are one of the oldest dog sports. One of the first sheepdog trials was held in New Zealand in 1867. There, shepherds and their dogs had 30 minutes to herd three sheep across the hilly land. A dog named Sweep came in first place.

Trials started to become popular in different regions. In the United States, the first herding trial marked Philadelphia's centennial year celebration in 1880. The winner, Oscar, was a black and tan collie from Scotland. He worked his flock of five sheep quickly and with

Shepherds have used corgis and their short-legged ancestors for centuries.

great skill. Oscar received several rounds of applause from his audience.

TOP uS TRIALS

Today many clubs host sheepdog trials in the United States. The AKC runs one of the biggest. This club's herding program began in 1989. It lets handlers choose from different courses. They also select which livestock to work. The most common choices are cattle, sheep, goats, or ducks. The AKC's competitive trials are designed for dogs that have prior herding experience.

Some clubs focus on a particular herding breed. The Australian Shepherd Club of America tests this breed's ability to handle stock, though it allows other herding breeds to participate too. It holds three different types of trials. These range from arena trials with set courses to farm and ranch trials with large herds and chores like those seen on a real ranch, such as loading trailers. The United States Border Collie Handlers' Association hosts trials across the country. Border collies herd sheep or cattle at these events.

Some animals may challenge herding dogs more than others.

Top Border collies and their handlers compete at the Soldier Hollow Classic Sheepdog Championship. This four-day event is challenging. Teams from around the world compete. Border collies work up to 400 yards (365 m) from their handlers. First they gather wild-range ewes. *Wild range* means sheep that have never been worked by a dog before. These sheep won't willingly do everything a dog asks, which makes them challenging. The dogs bring the sheep down a mountainside and through gates. Finally, the dogs need to separate some sheep and place them in a pen. From start to finish, teams must complete the course in 13 minutes or less.

RAISING A SHEEPDOG

Herding dogs are born with the instinct to herd. However, they still need training to encourage this natural ability. One of a trainer's first steps is to introduce the puppy to new places and people. This helps the pup gain confidence.

Herding requires teamwork between dog and handler. The dog should enjoy working with a partner. The handler should teach the dog to combine its instincts and training. Together, the team will face challenges and build confidence.

A herding pup needs to learn basic skills and commands. Training sessions teach the puppy to walk on

THE BORDER COLLIE

Some people consider the Border collie the best breed for herding. For centuries people bred the Border collie for its working ability, not appearance. When the AKC recognized the Border collie for conformation shows in 1994, many owners were upset. They worried that the shows would cause breeders to emphasize appearance over working ability. Many breeders do not register with the AKC for this reason.

a leash without pulling and to follow commands such as *sit*, *down*, *stay*, *come*, and *leave it*. The trainer should keep sessions short and end on a positive note. Treats and praise should be used to reward the puppy.

Some herding skills combine multiple commands. For example, the trainer might tell the pup to stay. Then the trainer tosses a favorite toy and instructs the puppy to chase it. Finally, the trainer gets the pup to stop on command. After learning basic commands, the puppy will meet livestock. The first step is to visit a farm or ranch. There the pup can watch sheep or cows in pens. The handler can observe the puppy to see how it reacts.

Then the pup should be trained in a manner that will boost its confidence. Dogs new to herding start with livestock that are easy to control. These animals do not challenge the dog. Herding teams also begin in a small field. They can build up their skills and abilities slowly. Handlers work beginner dogs at short distances, no more than approximately 25 feet (7.6 m) away. At the same time, handlers give their dogs space to move around the stock.

Puppies often show herding instincts the first time they meet livestock.

With patience and practice, dogs learn to take charge of the stock while looking to their handlers for guidance.

Many people prepare their dogs for trials by training with an instructor. The instructor usually has experience competing in trials. The dogs learn many important commands:

- *Come-bye* means to go clockwise around the stock.

- *Away* means to go counterclockwise around the stock.

- *Walk on* tells the dog to walk closer to the stock.

- *Look back* indicates the dog must return for a missed animal.

- *Steady* means to slow down.

- *Lie down* means to stop and lie flat on the ground.

When a dog hears *that'll do*, it stops its work and returns to the handler. Handlers use these commands to direct the dog's position, which in turn affects the direction the stock is headed. Some trainers may use different commands or whistles for these same skills.

TESTS
AND TRIALS

Dogs that compete in herding trials need stamina. When a herding dog gets tired, it is less able to outthink the stock. This can lead to mistakes such as leaving an animal behind. Owners can keep their animals fit by practicing herding regularly. Other exercises such as playing ball, swimming, or jogging can also help keep herding dogs in shape.

Herding dogs need to be able to run for long periods of time.

TESTS

The AKC offers two tests for dogs that aren't quite ready for trials. The herding instinct test is the simplest. It is designed to test the natural herding ability of dogs six months and older. This test is noncompetitive. The dog must show interest in herding livestock. It should either go around, gather together, and fetch the stock toward the handler, or drive them ahead of the handler. After passing two separate tests, the dog will be awarded a certificate.

The herding test is a bit more difficult than the instinct test. At the start, the dog must stay in position until released. Then it must change direction twice while controlling the movement of the livestock. The test ends with a stop and recall. The dog is allowed 10 minutes to complete the herding test. It will earn an HT title added to the end of its name.

The pre-trial test is the most challenging test. Again, the dog has 10 minutes to qualify. After a stay, the dog must control the stock by fetching or driving. It must guide the stock through four gates. The dog must stop once on the course and once while the handler opens the pen gate. Then it must pen the sheep to earn a PT title.

HERDING TRIALS

Unlike the tests, AKC trials are competitive. These trials show that herding breeds can move and fetch livestock,

In a herding trial, a dog may have to herd sheep into a small pen.

the jobs for which they were originally bred. The trials also stress teamwork between the handler and dog.

There are three different levels at an AKC herding trial: started, intermediate, and advanced. The handler can choose from three different courses, or do all three. Course A resembles a farm or ranch. It tests how the herding dog moves between tasks. Course B is an open field. It tests how the dog controls and moves stock in a wider area. Course C looks like a pasture. It tests how the dog tends a flock of sheep in an unfenced area.

In both tests and trials, handlers can be any age. They just need to be able to control their dogs. Dogs start a herding trial with 100 points. The judges deduct points as errors are made. The dog must end up with at least 60 points to receive a qualifying score. At the end of the trials, titles are awarded to dogs with the required number of qualifying scores. In AKC, the lowest level needs only three qualifying scores. The next title requires eight more qualifying scores.

A DAY AT A HERDING TRIAL

The parking lot is filled with cars and campers on the morning of the herding trial. Handlers and their herding dogs arrive hours before the first run at 8:00 a.m. So do most of the spectators.

This trial is held on a working farm. Months before the trial, handlers sent in their entries along with a fee for each dog. Competition was fierce. Only 50 runs were allowed on this day. The club hosting the trial had already drawn entries for running order.

Dogs that herd ducks need to be gentle.

Volunteers make certain that everything goes smoothly before, during, and after the trial. They help set up and tear down equipment. They guide cars in the parking lot and admit people at the gate. Some volunteers help out at the sheep pen. Others make announcements. One assists the judges.

THE COMPETITION

Herding dogs and their handlers wait for their turns in the ring. The dogs range in age from nine months through seniors, who may be more than 10 years old. Some heel on leash, taking bathroom breaks or slurping water. A few cool off in wading pools. Others rest in their crates beneath tents and trees.

Dogs running the courses herd sheep. At the start of each run, the sheep are rotated with a fresh flock. That way the livestock are not overworked by the eager dogs. One by one, teams of handlers and their dogs enter

TREIBBALL

Treibball is a fun sport from Germany that dogs of all ages and sizes can play. Instead of herding sheep, the dog herds a flock of big exercise balls. The dog has 15 minutes to push eight balls across a field and into a goal as the handler gives cues.

Dogs that herd cattle at trials need to be bold and tough.

the course. Handlers guide dogs with their voices and whistles, giving commands.

Depending on the class, dogs start out with 90 to 110 points. For a perfect score, the dog needs to get behind the sheep. Then it has to gather the sheep and start them moving. Next the dog needs to retrieve the sheep to the handler. Then it has to drive the sheep through gates and put them in the pen. Finally, the dog needs to bring the sheep to a ring and split off one sheep from the flock.

Judges watch the dogs carefully to evaluate each part of their runs. They deduct points for mistakes. For example, dogs lose points for stopping and starting instead of moving the sheep smoothly along the course. Judges disqualify any dogs that bit sheep.

When the trial ends at 5:00 p.m., judges award points to decide ranking. The top dogs receive ribbons. First place is a blue ribbon. At this competition, the top scoring

HERDING STYLES

Different breeds herd livestock in distinct ways. Australian cattle dogs guide with sharp barks and nipping at heels. Border collies get in front of animals and silently stare them down. The Australian Kelpie uses both of these herding methods and sometimes will jump on the backs of sheep.

Dogs are tired but happy after a long day herding.

senior dog receives a special silver award. Cash prizes are rare, but a few trials also offer those to winners. Regardless of how they score, the tired handlers and their dogs head home to rest. They will continue to train and grow their herding skills. Another herding trial is on the horizon.

GLOSSARY

breed

Domestic animals that have common ancestors and physical and behavioral traits. Also, to keep and take care of animals in order to produce more of a particular kind.

conformation

A competition that judges how well a dog matches its breed's physical standard.

disqualify

To make a contestant ineligible for a prize because of violations of the rules.

ewe

A female sheep.

herd

A group of animals. Also, to get animals to move as a group in the direction you want them to go.

instinct

A strong natural impulse.

noncompetitive

Not involving competition.

predator

An animal that hunts, kills, and eats other animals.

recall

A signal to return.

stamina

The ability to do something for a long period of time.

sync

A state in which two or more people or things move together at the same time and speed.

trait

An inherited characteristic.

trial

An event where dogs compete, are judged, and receive scores.

MORE INFORMATION

ONLINE RESOURCES

To learn more about herding dogs, visit **abdobooklinks.com**. These links are routinely monitored and updated to provide the most current information available.

BOOKS

Furstinger, Nancy. *Dogs*. Minneapolis, MN: Abdo Publishing, 2014.

Pearson, Marie. *Agility Dogs*. Minneapolis, MN: Abdo Publishing, 2019.

Sundance, Kyra. *101 Dog Tricks, Kids Edition: Fun and Easy Activities, Games, and Crafts*. Beverly, MA: Quarry, 2014.

INDEX

ABOUT THE AUTHOR

Nancy Furstinger has been speaking up for animals since she learned to talk. She is the author of nearly 100 books, including many on her favorite topic: animals! She has been a feature writer for a daily newspaper, a managing editor of trade and consumer magazines, and an editor at two children's book publishing houses. She shares her home with big dogs, house rabbits, and a chinchilla (all rescued), and she volunteers and fosters pets for several animal organizations.